The Story of Communication

by
Betty Bacon

illustrated by
Sean O'Neill

PEARSON

Scott
Foresman

Editorial Offices: Glenview, Illinois • Parsippany, New Jersey • New York, New York
Sales Offices: Needham, Massachusetts • Duluth, Georgia • Glenview, Illinois
Coppell, Texas • Ontario, California • Mesa, Arizona

If you want to talk with someone who is far away, you can call them on the telephone. But what did people do before there were telephones?

People have always communicated with others who were far away. They found many ways to do that. Let's learn about some of the early ways.

Smoke

Some people used smoke to send messages. They would wave blankets over a smoky fire. Puffs of smoke would rise into the air. Different numbers of smoke puffs meant different things. For example, one puff of smoke might mean danger!

People far away saw the smoke and could read the messages.

Some groups of people used drums to send messages. The sounds the drums made could be heard far away.

People played drums to tell others when hunts or parties were going to happen.

Drums

Drum and smoke signals could send messages quickly and far away. But the messages couldn't be very long.

People could carry longer messages from place to place. Once people could write, they began to send written notes.

Later, people started sending messages in letters through the mail.

Before there were trains or cars, people used horses to take mail from one place to another.

Mail

Even though people ran or rode fast horses, the mail took a long time to get from one place to the next.

Pigeons are small, fast birds that can be taught to fly from one place to another. People would strap a small note to a pigeon's leg. The pigeon would then fly with the note.

Pigeon

In 1844, the first telegraph message was sent by a man named Samuel Morse. This was a new way to communicate.

Using electricity, Morse made a machine that sent beeps from one place to another. The beeps stood for the alphabet. For example, one fast beep and one slow beep meant the letter A.

Telegraph

Telephone

Then, a man named Alexander Bell tried to make a different machine. He knew a lot about science. He thought he could send spoken words, not just beeps, through electric wires.

In 1876, Bell built the first telephone, a machine that sent spoken words by electricity. Now people could talk to each other right away!

Telephones have changed a lot since Bell's first phone. Now, there are different kinds of telephones. What kinds of phones can you see in the picture?

Computer

Using the telephone is a fast way to communicate to people far away. What about a computer? A lot of people send messages to each other through their computers. Have you ever done that?

Over the years, people have found many ways to communicate over great distances. Soon, we may learn even more.